I0151008

Potions, Herbs, Oils & Brews: The Reference Guide for Potions, Herbs, Incense, Oils, Ointments, and Brews

By: Kristina Benson

Potions, Herbs, Oils & Brews: The Reference Guide for
Potions, Herbs, Incense, Oils, Ointments, and Brews

ISBN: 978-1-60332-034-1

Copyright© 2008 Equity Press all rights reserved. No part
of this publication may be reproduced, stored in a retrieval
system, or transmitted in any form or by any means
(electronic, mechanical, photocopying, recording or
otherwise) without either the prior written permission of
the publisher or a license permitting restricted copying in
the United States or abroad.

The scanning, uploading and distribution of this book via
the internet or via any other means without the permission
of the publisher is illegal and punishable by law. Please
purchase only authorized electronic editions, and do not
participate in or encourage piracy of copyrighted materials.

The programs in this book have been included for
instructional value only. They have been tested with
care but are not guaranteed for any particular purpose.
The publisher does not offer any warranties or
representations does not accept any liabilities with
respect to the programs.

Trademarks: All trademarks are the property of their
respective owners. Equity Press is not associated with any
product or vender mentioned in this book.

Printed in the United States of America

Table of Contents

GENERAL CORRESPONDENCES

When performing a spell or designing your own perfumes and scents, it is important to know what corresponds with what. The following list should help you decide which fragrances to pair with which color candles and what types of incense. This is helpful not only for spells, but for providing a harmonious atmosphere in which to live and do your work.

The oils, incense, gemstones, and fragrances are listed by purpose here.

Change Your Luck

Oil: lotus
Herb: basil or pepper
Incense: frankincense
Gemstones: carnelian
Candle Colors: green

Attract Material Wealth

Oil: bergamot or cinnamon
Herb: nutmeg
Incense: cinnamon
Stone: agate or garnet
Metal: gold
Candle Colors: green or gold

Increase Personal Power

Oil: ylang ylang

Herb: sandalwood or patchouli

Incense: frankincense or pine

Stone: agate, jasper, black obsidian

Candle: red

Conquer Fear

Oil: musk or sandalwood

Herbs: sage

Incense: allspice, musk

Stones: amber, black obsidian, garnet

Candle: red

Attract Success

Oil: peppermint or spearmint

Herb: ginger or rosemary

Incense: ginger or rosemary

Stones: black obsidian

Metal: silver or gold

Candle: gold or orange

Inspire Creativity

Oil: lilac, jasmine, or rose

Herb: rose petals

Incense: lilac, lotus or rose

Stone: black onyx, lapis, turquoise

Candle: violet or yellow

Overcome Bad Habits

Oil: cedar or peppermint

Herbs: basil, bay laurel, peppermint, sandalwood

Incense: cedar, peppermint

Stones: jet, topaz

Candles: purple

Inspire Peace

Oil: jasmine, chamomile

Herb: vanilla bean

Incense: allspice, cedar, patchouli

Stones: onyx

Candle: pink, light blue

Settle Bad Energy

Oil: patchouli

Herb: sage

Incense: patchouli or amber

Stones: hematite, agate

Candle: white, purple

Release Bad Energies or People from Your Life

Oil: lilac and lavender

Herb: lemon grass, sage

Incense: patchouli or cedar

Stones: aventurine, jade,

Candle: black

Acceptance

Oil: gardenia, jasmine, neroli

Herb: frankincense

Incense: rose, orange, musk

Stones: sard and amazonite

Candle: brown

General Antidepressant

Oil: orange

Herb: St. Johns wort

Incense: jasmine or rose

Stones: amethyst, topaz

Candle: gold, lt. blue

Consecrate a Space or Tool

Oil: lotus

Herb: sage

Incense: lotus or sandalwood

Stone: bloodstone, black onyx, jade

Candle: white or purple

Peaceful Spiritual Separation, Letting Go

Oil: patchouli, sandalwood

Herb: lemon verbena, lemon grass

Incense: patchouli, musk

Stone: sodalite, chalcedony

Candle: light blue

Celebrate a Birth

Oil: rose, almond, cocoa
Herb: rose petals
Incense: frankincense or myrrh
Stone: lapis
Candle: pink

In Memory of the Dead

Oil: patchouli
Herb: patchouli, honey
Incense: patchouli or lotus
Stones: lapis lazuli
Candle: lavender, light blue

Giving Thanks

Oil: lotus or frankincense
Herb: sage
Incense: frankincense, myrrh
Stones: amethyst, iolite
Candle: white or gold

General Healing

Oil: carnation, myrrh, lavender

Herb: raspberry leaves, chamomile

Incense: lotus or lavender

Stone: amber, turquoise

Candle: green, gold, lt. blue

Regain Health

Oil: carnation

Herbs: sandalwood, peppercorn

Incense: carnation, rose, orange

Stones: bloodstone, jade

Candle: green

Purge Bad Energy From a Relationship

Oil: ylang ylang, rose, jasmine

Herb: bay leaf

Incense: frangipani or pine

Stone: moonstone, opal, pyrite

Candle: indigo

Rebuild an Unhappy marriage or Relationship

Oil: rose

Herb: rose petals

Incense: apple blossom, allspice, sandalwood

Stone: agate, amethyst, lapis, diamond

Metal: gold

Candle: pink

Win the Love of a Man

Oil: vanilla or apple

Herb: ginger

Incense: vanilla or ylang

Stone: lodestone, aventurine, malachite

Candle: red

Win the Love of a Woman

Oil: musk

Herb: rose petals

Incense: jasmine or rose

Stone: coral, lodestone, rose quartz

Candle: pink

Attract Love (Man or Woman)

Oil: musk

Herb: rose petals

Incense: musk, patchouli

Stone: moss agate, clear quartz crystal, lapis, rose quartz

Candle: green, pink

Release an Unwanted Admirer or Lover

Oil: patchouli

Herb: lemon verbena or cayenne pepper

Incense: patchouli or rue

Stone: spectrolite, jade, clear quartz, agate, malachite

Candle: black

Rid Yourself of Negatives

Oil: pine

Herb: sage

Incense: cedar or sandalwood

Stone: 2 pieces. Hematite or smoky quartz

Candle: purple, black, silver, gold

Release from Psychic Attack

Oil: patchouli, frankincense

Herb: patchouli, sage

Incense: cedar or myrrh

Stone: smoky quartz, turquoise, black obsidian, amethyst

Candle: black, silver

Remove Negative Vibrations or Spirits from a Home

Oil: vetiver or yarrow

Herb: sage, patchouli, ginger

Incense: frankincense, myrrh or patchouli

Stone: agate, clear quartz crystal, bloodstone

Candle: black, silver

Remove Negative Vibrations or Spirits from a Person or Animal

Oil: vetiver or patchouli
Herb: vetiver or patchouli
Incense: frankincense, myrrh, patchouli
Stone: agate, clear quartz crystal, black onyx, black obsidian
Candle: black, silver

Bring Pressure on an Adversary

Oil: pine
Herb: bay laurel, clove, sage, pepper
Incense: dragons blood, pine, patchouli, sandalwood
Stone: aquamarine, topaz
Candle: orange, indigo

Uncross a Person

Oil: cedar or patchouli

Herb: dragons blood, nutmeg, wormwood

Incense: cedar, myrrh, patchouli, sandalwood, honey

Stone: honey stone, mica, clear quartz crystal, black
obsidian, black onyx,

Candle: purple, white

Protect Someone from Abuse or Bad Energy

Oil: frankincense, sage

Herb: bay laurel, frankincense, rosemary

Incense: dragons blood, frankincense, patchouli

Stone: jasper, lapis, smoky quartz, black obsidian

Candle: black

Enhance Spiritual Growth

Oil: lotus, jasmine

Herb: frankincense

Incense: lotus or sandalwood

Stone: amber, citrine, lapis, ruby, sapphire, jade

Candle: lavender, purple, white

Gain Spiritual Blessings

Oil: frankincense

Herb: frankincense

Incense: frankincense or lotus

Stone: amethyst, lapis, topaz, black tourmaline

Candle: blue, lavender, white

Strengthen Psychic Abilities

Oil: jasmine

Herb: wormwood, nutmeg, ginger or jasmine flowers

Incense: honeysuckle, mimosa or lotus

Stone: moss agate, moonstone, jet, blue topaz, purple tourmaline

Candle: silver, lavender, purple

POTIONS

INTRODUCTION

Love potions are in high demand and often brewed. There exists a fair amount of debate as to whether or not it is ethical to cast love spells or brew love potions. The nature and scope of this debate is too broad to be discussed here in great depth, however, to summarize: it is up to you to make sure that your intentions are pure and that you are not trying to force anyone into anything. Most agree that it does not violate the Wiccan Rede to merely attempt to appear more attractive to a potential lover. It may, however, violate the Rede, to try to force someone— particularly someone who is already in a committed relationship—to love you.

This said, before brewing your potions and ointments, examine your intentions and think hard on your motivations. Only you know what is best and right for you.

The following are some examples of love potions for more reading on Love Spells, Please buy a copy of Wiccan Love Spells written by Kristen Benson.

LOVE POTION NUMBER 1

Ingredients:

3 red apples
1 pinch cinnamon
1 pinch nutmeg
1 cup spring water
1 pinch sugar

As always, bless and concentrate the ingredients as well as the tools you will be using in order to prepare the potion. Slice the apples and place them in a saucepan. Sprinkle them with cinnamon and nutmeg. Pour enough water to submerge the apples and add a small sprinkling of sugar.

Stir clockwise on low heat. Focus on your goal, and invoke whichever goddess pleases you. You may wish to chant a spell or incantation.

Bring the apples to a low simmer, and let them sit for about an hour. Then, take the pan off the heat and let the contents cool. When everything has cooled down, place the apples and liquid into a jar—preferably a dark one—and store in the fridge. Use a few drops of it as cologne or perfume for at least four days.

LOVE POTION TEA

Ingredients:

1 pinch rosemary
2 or 3 whole cloves
3 pinches thyme
3 pinches nutmeg
3 fresh mint leaves
6 fresh rose petals
1 large piece of lemon peel
3 cups pure spring water
honey to taste

For best results, brew this tea on a waxing moon and on a Friday.

Place all ingredients in a consecrated tea kettle, along with hot spring water. Let it steep, and then add a teaspoon or so of honey.

Before drinking, say:

> *By light of moon I brew this tea*
> *So that may _____ desire me.*

Drink some and say,

> *By light of moon, now hear my plea*
> *So_____ desires me.*

On the following Friday, brew another pot of the love potion tea and give some to the person you want to love you. Make sure he or she drinks at least a cup. You should see results within a week.

PERFUMES, OINTMENTS, AND OILS

INTRODUCTION

The following perfumes are not to be taken internally! They are to be carefully blended and applied to the pulse points. For best results, choose organic or high-quality oils. Store them in amber or dark bottles in a cool place.

OIL CORRESPONDENCES

This will come in handy if you would like to modify the below recipes, or make your own oils.

Love: Bergamot, gardenia, jasmine, lavender, rose.

Lust: basil, cinnamon, ginger, neroli, sandalwood, ylang ylang, patchouli

Prosperity: almond, bergamot, honeysuckle, mint, peony, sage

Healing: Raspberry, carnation, mimosa, rosemary, sandalwood, chamomile, lavender

Protection: Sage, basil, frankincense, lavender, myrrh, cinnamon, pennyroyal

Luck: all spice, nutmeg, orange, violet,

Business/Money: Chrysanthemum, cinnamon, mint, peony.

Success: Geranium, cinnamon, bergamot, clove, ginger, lemon balm.

Happiness: Vanilla, almond, lavender, Lilly of the valley, marjoram, cherry

Sleep: chamomile, lavender, violet.

Vitality: bay, carnation, pennyroyal, pepper, peppermint

Peace: jasmine lavender, gardenia, passion flower, skullcap.

RECIPES

LUST POTION

Ingredients:

6 drops of Patchouli oil

6 drops of Rose oil

6 drops of Clove oil

6 drops of Nutmeg oil

6 drops of Amber oil

6 drops Vanilla oil

Mix these oils and wear them as a perfume on your wrists and solar plexus. This was designed to attract a man, not a woman, by the way.

LOVE ME MADLY SPELL

Ingredients:

1 cup orange juice from blood oranges
tiny pinch of lemon peel
tiny pinch nutmeg

This can work on either men or women, and it is perfect for people who are already in a relationship but want to take it to the next step. Just make this drink and have your lover drink it in your presence!

WEALTH POTION

Ingredients:

2 drops sandalwood oil

1 drop patchouli oil

1 drop clove oil

1 drop nutmeg oil

You will also need:

silk

a green candle

parchment

a pen with green, silver, or gold ink.

Athame

Combine the oils together and soak up the oils on a piece of silk, which you will place on your altar.

On the parchment draw a money symbol such as a dollar, pound, or yen sign. You could also draw the prosperity run, or glue the appropriate tarot card to the parchment. Take a knife and carve the word "Prosperity" into the wax. Rub the candle with the silk. Light it and let it burn for a half hour. Do this every night, and sleep with the silk under your pillow. It should take about a week.

PRIESTESS OF THE MOON PERFUME

Ingredients:

3 drops rose oil
3 drops vanilla oil
3 drops sandalwood oil
1 ounce grapeseed oil

Blend the oils in a bottle and shake to mix it. Ideally, the oils should be stored in a dark or amber bottle. This perfume is best used for the drawing down of the moon.

EARTH MOTHER PERFUME

Ingredients:

patchouli oil
sandalwood oil
jasmine oil

Blend in equal parts, bottle and shake well.

SUN ENERGY PERFUME

Ingredients:

Cinnamon Oil
Clove oil
Ylang-Ylang Oil
Black pepper Oil

Blend equal parts, bottle and shake well.

PERFUMED LAVENDER OINTMENT

Ingredients:

4 ounces beeswax
1/2 cup sweet almond oil
1 tablespoon Lavender essential oil

In a double boiler, combine the beeswax and the almond oil and heat until the beeswax has melted.

Remove from heat. Stir in the lavender and keep stirring for about a minute. Pour into containers and let cool completely until solid. When the ointment has cooled, use it as a perfume, and apply to the pulse points.

ROSE WATER

Ingredients:

1 cup distilled water

2 1/2 tablespoons top shelf vodka, OR filtered well-quality vodka

20 drops rose fragrance oil

1/2 cup rose flowers (fresh or dried will do)

Tools:

1 clean airtight container or jar

1 clean spoon

1 coffee filter or cheese cloth

1-2 airtight, amber or dark bottles to store the fragrance.

Fill the jar or container with the flower petals, and pour the water and vodka over the petals. Gently fold the petals into the water and vodka with a spoon. Add the essential oil and continue stirring. Seal container and set in cool, dark place for one week, stirring every few days. One week later, strain liquid through coffee filter or cheese cloth and discard the petals. Bottle the lavender water immediately.

It can be stored in a dark bottle and kept up to one year.

FLORAL PERFUME

Ingredients:

2 tablespoons fresh rose petals

2 tablespoons fresh jasmine flowers

1 lemon peel, grated

1 tablespoon fresh Rosemary

1 tablespoon fresh Peppermint

2 cups water

1 1/4 cups vodka

Place the flowers, peel, and herbs in a small saucepan and cover with the water. Simmer on low heat for 5 minutes but do not bring to a rolling boil. Cool completely and add the vodka. Pour the mixture into a clean container with a tight-fitting lid and place in a cool, dry location for 2 weeks.

Two weeks later, strain off all solids and bottle your cologne in a dark bottle.

LADY OF THE LAKE OIL

Ingredients:

1/4 ounce almond oil,
15 drops orange oil
 5 drops rose oil,
1 drop cinnamon oil,
4 drops thyme oil,
14 drops chamomile oil,
2 drops ginger oil

Combine all oils and shake vigorously.

Store in an airtight, amber or dark bottle.

Use on pulse points as a perfume or cologne.

STAR OIL

Ingredients:

1/4 ounce grapeseed oil

10 drops lemon oil

7 drops jasmine oil

7 drops rosemary oil

17 drops chamomile oil

4 drops sage oil

Combine all oils and shake vigorously.

Store in an airtight, amber or dark bottle.

Use on pulse points as a perfume or cologne.

FULL MOON OIL

Ingredients:

13 drops of sandalwood essential oil

9 drops of vanilla essential oil or extract

3 drops of mango essential oil

1 drop amber essential oil

Mix prior to a full moon.

Charge in a clear container in the light of the full moon. Use to anoint candles or yourself for full moon rituals.

Remember: Move the potion to an amber bottle for storage.

PROTECTION POTION

Ingredients:

2-4 Cups of Spring Water, as a base

1 Tbsp. Powdered Iron or Iron Shavings

1 tsp. Vervain

1 tbsp sage oil

1 pinch hair of a coyote, fox, or wolf

This potion is not to be taken internally! Use it to consecrate an object or space.

SLEEP SPELL & OIL

Ingredients:

1/2 oz grapeseed or apricot kernel oil

12 drops chamomile oil

3 drops lavender

3 drops eucalyptus oil

Mix the oils and use as a perfume just before going to sleep.

LOVE AND ADMIRATION OIL

Ingredients:

10 drops patchouli
2 drops jasmine
1 drop of ylang ylang

Mix the oils and leave the bottle where the full moonlight can strike it for three nights. Do not let the sunlight touch it. Bring it inside before the sun rises.

When you remove the bottle, replace it with

1 rose petal
1 piece rose quartz
5 almonds

Leave them in a place where the Sun can see them, making sure to move them before moonlight can strike them. On the fourth day, mix together the two sets of ingredients and leave in a dark place. Wear the oils and rose quartz etc is a sachet. Carry it in your purse or pocket when you wish to draw love and admiration to yourself.

LUST POTION

Ingredients:

6 drops of Sandalwood oil
6 drops of Rose oil
6 drops of Clove oil
6 drops of Nutmeg oil

Wear as a perfume whenever you'll be in the presence of the person you're trying to attract.

ATTRACTION OIL

Ingredients:

7 drops rose oil
7 drops orange oil
1 clove
7 drops vanilla

Wear as a perfume and store in an airtight amber bottle.

APHRODITE OIL

Ingredients:

3 drops Jasmine

3 drops Rose

1 drop Lavender

2 drops Vanilla

1 drop Patchouli

1 drop Bergamot

On a Friday night blend the oils. This oil should only be worn by women wishing to attract men.

PROTECTION OIL

Ingredients:

1 tbsp grapeseed oil

4 drops cinnamon oil

4 drops vanilla oil

2 drops sandalwood oil

Use on yourself or to consecrate items or a space.

PROSPERITY POTION

Ingredients:

One part sandalwood oil
One part sage oil
One part clove bud oil
One part amber oil
One part nutmeg oil

Rub the oil on a piece of jade to carry in a sachet or pocket for extra strong effect.

SEAWOMAN OIL

Ingredients:

1 pinch Seaweed or one strip of dried seaweed
1 Seashell
A pinch of Sea Salt
1 cup sea water

Mix ingredients and use to anoint candles, talismans, amulets, or other objects.

GENERAL ANOINTING OIL

Ingredients:

1 handful mint or spearmint leaves
1 handful thyme
1 pinch ginger
1 oz grapeseed or apricot kernel oil
4 oz beeswax

Melt the beeswax in a double boiler and add the leaves and oil. Strain the leaves out eventually if you wish but it might be nice to have chunks of leaves and herbs in the ointment. Cool and use to anoint sacred objects, or yourself.

FULL MOON OIL

Ingredients:

13 drops of sandalwood essential oil

9 drops of vanilla essential oil or extract

3 drops jasmine oil

3 drops of jasmine essential oil

1 drop of rose essential oil

Mix prior to a full moon. Charge in a clear container or vial in the light of the full moon. Use to anoint candles or yourself for full moon rituals or just when you want to feel some of the moon's energy.

TRUTH OIL

Ingredients:

3 drops Sage

3 drops Lavender

 2 drops Pine

1 pinch marigold leaves

1 pinch nutmeg

Blend together and use to anoint objects, or yourself. It will inspire others around you to tell the truth.

BANISHING OIL

Ingredients:

½ oz apricot kernel oil

7 drops pepper oil or pinch of pepper (cayenne works best)

10 drops peppermint oil

12 drops of rue or rosemary oil

1 handful pine needles

1 bundle dried sage

1 black onyx stone

Simply mix the ingredients, and strain out the herbs after a week.

Do not anoint yourself with this oil as it is very strong.

Use it to sprinkle on a space or surface. As you do it, focus on the person or energies you wish to banish.

THIRD EYE OIL

Ingredients:

1 part amber oil
1 part vanilla oil
½ part cinnamon oil

Use this on your third eye. To make it more potent, store a small amethyst in the bottle along with it. Be careful, however, because it is potent and will irritate the mucous membranes.

HOLYDAY OIL

Ingredients:

1 part frankincense

1 part myrrh

1 part sage

½ part cinnamon

½ part lemon peel

¼ part ginger

Mix, and use for anointing.

SPRAY WITH OILS

Ingredients

1/4 cup high quality vodka

¼ cup rose water

3 tbsp almond oil

Pour all ingredients into a spray pump bottle and close. Shake the bottle until well mixed. Shake before each use.

HERBS

Herbs have many properties. They can heal spiritual and physical ailments. There will be a section on the manner in which herbs can heal physical afflictions, but the following details the manner in which herbs can control energies and manipulate the spirit. They are listed by purpose.

HERBS BY AILMENT:

ABUNDANCE: wheat, rye, barley

ACHIEVEMENT: rose, ginger, jasmine

ADDICTION-BREAK: fresh cut grass, cayenne pepper, alfalfa

ADDICTIONS-CURB: anise

AFFECTION-BONDS OF: carnation, marigold

AFTERLIFE, TO INSURE HAPPINESS IN: marjoram, neroli

ALL-WISE: goldenrod, ginkgo biloba

ANCESTORS-HONOR: cypress, laurel, bay

ANGER: alyssum, St John's wort to moderate

ANOINTING: acacia, almond, amber, apricot kernel, angelica, carnation, frankincense, high john jasmine, lavender, lily of the valley, lotus, myrrh, rose, rosemary, sage, vervain, wood aloe

APHRODISIAC: ambergris, apricot, basil, beet, cardinal flower, cinnamon, cubeb, dong quai, ginseng, lemon, musk, patchouli, vanilla beans, violet

POWER: bistort

PROJECTION: belladonna, cinnamon, dittany, mugwort

PROTECTION: anise, datura foxglove, lettuce, nutmeg, sage

STRENGTH: frankincense, ginseng, ginger

ATONEMENT: plantain, orange, laurel

ATTRACTION: jasmine, musk, rose, vanilla,
INCREASE: acorn, lemon verbena

AWAKEN: cayenne, ginger, ginseng, peppercorns

BALANCE: chamomile, jasmine, orange, rose, valerian

BANISH NEGATIVE/UNWANTED SPIRITS: cinnamon, copal

INVINCIBILITY: cayenne pepper, coffee dong quai, ginseng,

BEAUTY: avocado, belladonna, catnip, clover, cocoa, coffee, flax, ginseng, lavender, maidenhair, rose, yerba santa,

INCREASE: cowslip, ginger

BEWITCHMENT-GUARD AGAINST: nutmeg, wormwood

BLACK ARTS: belladonna, deadly nightshade, hellebore, hemlock, henbane, skullcap

BLESSING, HOUSE: rose, sage

BOLDNESS: basil, pepper, thyme

CALMING: chamomile, jasmine, juniper, lilac, valerian, violet

CAT MAGICK: catnip

CELIBACY, PROMOTE: camphor, chamomile, jasmine, lilac

CENTERING: clary sage

CHAKRAS-OPEN: patchouli, sandalwood

CHASTITY: camphor, chaste tree, coconut, cucumber, hawthorn, job's tears, lavender, pennyroyal, pineapple, sweet pea, vervain, wild lettuce, witch hazel

CLAIRVOYANCE: acacia, anise, bay, broom, dittany of crete, eyebright, hazel, honeysuckle, lettuce, lilac, marigold, moonwort, mugwort, nutmeg, rose, rowan, thyme, wormwood, yarrow

CLEANSING: alkanet, anise, asafetida avens, basil, bay, benzoin, birch, bloodroot, burdock, calamus, camphor, cedar, chamomile, cinnamon, citronella, clove, coconut, dragon's blood, elder, eucalyptus, euphorbia, fennel, feverfew, frankincense, heather, horseradish, hyssop, iris, juniper, lavender, lemon, lemon verbena, lemongrass, life everlasting, lime, lovage, marjoram, mimosa, mullein, musk, myrrh, neroli, oak, orange, parsley, peppermint, pepper tree, pine, plantain, rosemary, rue, saffron, sage, sagebrush, salt, sandalwood, shallot, Solomon's seal, thistle/holy, thyme, tobacco, turmeric, valerian, vervain, wood betony, woodruff, yucca

COLDS, WARD OFF: garlic, pepper, ginger

COMFORT: amber, chamomile, cypress, jasmine, rose

COMPASSION: apple, bergamot, orange

CONCENTRATION: ginkgo biloba, lemongrass

INCREASE: celery seed

CONFIDENCE: jasmine

CONFLICT, PREPARATION FOR: broom, ginger, ginseng,

CONFUSION-RELIEVE: high john

CONSCIOUS MIND: lavender

AWAKEN: benzoin

CONSCIOUSNESS-AWAKEN HIGHER: frankincense, vanilla

CONTROL: bayberry, honeysuckle-remove

COSMIC FORCE: yarrow

COURAGE: allspice, borage, clove, cohosh-black, columbine, dragon's blood, frankincense, mandrake, mullein, musk, nettle, ragweed, rose geranium, tea

DETERMINATION: allspice, dong quai, dragon's blood,

DEFENSE: angelica, basil, bay, bayberry, birch, broom, burdock, cinnamon-confers, cinquefoil, club moss, cypress, dill, dragon's blood, fern, feverfew, fir, frankincense, hawthorn, hazel, heather, holly, jasmine, juniper, marjoram, mistletoe(amulet), mugwort, mullein, oak, patchouli, pepper, pine, rosemary, rowan, rue, St. John's wort, thistle, vervain, wormwood, yarrow

DEMONS: AVERT/WARD OFF: mullein, yarrow

DESPAIR- EXPEL: betony

DESPAIR-OVERCOME: couch grass

DETERMINATION, COURAGE: allspice, dragon's blood, mullein, musk, rosemary

DEVOTION: honeysuckle, jasmine, lavender, rose, rosemary

DIVINATION: acacia, almond, anise, ash, bay, bistort, broom, camphor, chicory, cinnamon, cherry, citron, clove, corn, corn flowers, dandelion, datura, dodder, eyebright, fig, galangal, goldenrod, ground ivy, hazel, hibiscus, honeysuckle, horse chestnut, st. johns wort, juniper, kava-kava, lemon grass, lettuce, mace, marigold, mastic, meadow rue, meadowsweet, mugwort, mullein, nutmeg, olioliuqui, orange, orris, pansy, patchouli, peppermint, pomegranate, roots, rose-red, rosemary, sandalwood, san pedro, star anise, thyme, wild cherry bark, wild lettuce, willow bark, witch hazel, wormwood, yarrow

DREAMS: chamomile, lavender, poppy,

DOWSING RODS: witch hazel

DRAGON ENERGY: hyssop, snapdragon

DREAMS: ambergris, ground ivy, valerian

DURATION: dandelion

EARTHLY DESIRES: .apple, beet, ginger, rose

ELOQUENCE: aspen

ELVES-MISCHIEVOUS PROTECT FROM: mugwort

EMOTIONS-WARM: nettle

EMOTIONAL PAIN- OVERCOME: blueberry, dandelion, raspberry,

EMPOWERMENT: cocoa, coffee, ephedra, ginger,

ENCHANTMENT: basil, bluebell

ENDURANCE: cayenne, oak, ginseng

ENLIGHTENMENT: amber, sandalwood

ENERGY: allspice, bay, cinnamon, cocoa, coffee, dong quai, dragon's blood, ephedra frankincense, ginseng, grapefruit, holly, lotus, musk, oak, peppermint, rosemary, yarrow

EUPHORIA: bergamot, cinnamon, nutmeg, ylang-ylang

EYE WARD AGAINST: ash

EXORCISM: angelica, arbutus, asafetida, avens, basil, bean, birch, boneset, broom, buckthorn, cedar, clove, clover, copal, cumin, devils bit, frankincense, fumitory, garlic, galangal, heliotrope, horehound, horseradish, job's tears, st johns wort, juniper, lavender, leek, lilac, mallow, mistletoe, mullein, myrrh, nettle, onion, peach, peony, pepper, pepper-cayenne, peppermint, rosemary, rue, sagebrush, snapdragon, sloe, Solomon's seal, thistle, tamarisk, turmeric, vervain, vetivert, violet, witch grass, wormwood, yarrow

EYESIGHT: beet, carrot, cornflower

FERTILITY: acorn, agaric, banana, basil, bistort, bodhi, caraway seed, carrot, catnip, chickweed, corn flowers, cuckoo-flower, cucumber, cyclamen, daffodil, dock, fig, geranium, grape, hawthorn, hazel, horsetail, lemon balm-

increases, mandrake, mistletoe, mullein, mustard, myrtle, nuts, oak, olive, orange palm-date, patchouli, peach, pine nuts, pomegranate, rose, rosemary, rice, spikenard, sunflower, sweet violet, walnut, wheat

FIDELITY: chili pepper, clover, ivy, coriander, licorice, nutmeg, rhubarb, rye, skullcap, yerba mate

FIERCENESS: cayenne, coffee, cinnamon, ephedra, ginseng, dong quai

FIND LOST OBJECTS: neroli

FIVE-FOLD STAR OF REBIRTH: apples

FOCUS: coffee, ginkgo biloba, lavender

FORTUNE-GOOD: see "luck, good fortune"

GAMBLING LUCK: rose, gardenia

GARDEN MAGICK: apple blossom, cinnamon grape

GHOSTS:BANISH: musk, patchouli, sage

GOOD SPIRITS ONLY ENTER: allspice, Irish moss,

GRACE-OBTAIN: periwinkle, violet

GRIEF-RELIEF: aloe

GROUNDING: almond, cedar, hazelnut, pine, patchouli, sandalwood

GROWTH: clover, red clover, patchouli

GUARD: pennyroyal

HAPPINESS: apple blossom, basil, bayberry, catnip, cedar, cinnamon, cocoa, cypress, fir, geranium-rose, hawthorn berry, high john-chase away the blues, hyacinth, jasmine, St. John's wort lavender, lemon, lilac, lily of the valley, loosestrife-purple, pomegranate lotus, marjoram, meadowsweet, neroli, orange, patchouli, purslane, rose, rosemary, saffron, sesame, strawberry, thyme, valerian

HARVEST: acorn, apple, blackberry, blueberry

HEART: lemon balm-

IMPOTENCY-TREAT: cinnamon, beets, blueberries. honey

INFERTILITY: walnut

INTUITION-STRENGTHEN: yarrow

JEALOUSY: garlic

KUNDALINI ENERGY: sandalwood

LONGEVITY: alfalfa, cypress, lavender, linden, lemon, lemon balm, life everlasting, maple, oak, orange, parsley, peach, raspberry leaves, ☐rosemary, sage, tansy, wheat grass

LOVE, GENERAL: aloe, apple blossom, apricot, avocado, avens, beet, birch, bloodroot, brazil nut, chamomile, cherry, cherry wood, chestnut, chickweed, clove, clover, cohosh-black, coltsfoot, columbine, copal, coriander, crocus, cubeb, cumin, daffodil, damiana, devils bit, dill, dogbane, elecampane, elm, endive, eryngo, fern, fig, frankincense, frangipani,, gardenia, gentian, ginseng, goldenrod, grains of paradise, heather, hemp, hibiscus, honeysuckle, house leek, hyacinth, indian paint brush, joe pye weed, lady's mantle, lemon verbena, lettuce, licorice, little john, lime, liverwort, magnolia, male fern, mallow, mandrake, maple, marjoram, mastic, mimosa, mint, moonwort, neroli, nuts, oak moss, ommak, orange, orchid, papaya, patchouli, pea, pear, peach, peppermint, periwinkle, pimento, pistachio, prickly ash, plumaria, primrose, purslane, quince, quassia, raspberry, rowan berry, rue, saffron, san pedro, sarsaparilla, savory, senna, snakeroot, southern wood, spearmint, spiderwort, spikenard, stephanotis, strawberry, sugar cane, sumbul, tamarind, tansy, thyme, tormentil, vervain, violet leaf, wheat, wild cherry bark, wild lettuce, wild rose, willow bark, witch grass, wood aloes, yerba mate, yohimbe

LOYALTY: primrose, rosemary

LUCK/FORTUNE-GOOD: alfalfa, aloe, apple, ash, bamboo, banyan, basil, bayberry, be-still, bluebell, cabbage, calamus, caper, cascara sagrada, catnip, cedar, chamomile, china berry, cinchona, cinnamon, cinquefoil, corn flowers, cubeb, cuckoo-flower, corn, cotton, daisy, daffodil, dandelion, dill, devils shoestring, dragon's blood, eryngo, fern, frankincense, galangal, grains of paradise, hazel, heal all, heather, holly, house leek, huckleberry, honeysuckle, ivy, jasmine, kava-kava, linden, lotus, male fern, mint, moss, nuts, oak, orange persimmon, pineapple, pomegranate, poppy seed, purslane, rose, snakeroot, rue, straw, sumbul, spikenard, star anise, strawberry, tonka beans, vetivert, vervain, violet, wood aloe, wood rose, yellow dock

LUST: ambergris, avocado, bergamot, caraway cardamom, carrot, cattail, celery, cinnamon, civet, clove, clover (red), cumin, cyclamen, daisy, damiana, deerstongue, devils bit, dill, dulse, endive, eryngo, garlic, galangal, ginger, ginseng, grains of paradise, hibiscus, honey, lemongrass, licorice, magnolia, maguey, mastic, mint, nettle(inducing), patchouli, pear, peppermint, periwinkle, radish, rosemary, saffron, sesame, snakeroot-black, southern wood, stephanotis, sugar cane, tuberose, vanilla, vetch, violet leaf,, witch grass, yerba mate, yohimbe □

MAGICKAL POISON: belladonna, hellebore, hemlock, henbane

MAGICKAL SPACE-PURIFY: frankincense, sage

MALE SEXUALITY: acorn, yohimbe

MARRIAGE: ivy, mistletoe, neroli, yarrow

MEDITATION: acacia, angelica, anise seeds, bay, bodhi, chamomile, eucalyptus, gotu kola, hemp, jasmine, lavender, lotus, magnolia, myrrh, nutmeg, wisteria

AID: elecampane

DEEP: nag champa,

DEEPEN: myrrh

MENTAL ABILITIES: ginkgo biloba, spearmint

MONEY: alfalfa, almond, bayberry, blackberry, bergamot mint, blue flag, bladderwrack, broom, bromeliad, bryony, buckwheat, calamus, cascara sagrada, cashew, cinquefoil, clove, clover, comfrey, corn, dill, dock, elder, fenugreek, flax, fumitory, galangal, goldenrod, golden seal, grains of paradise, grape, heal all, heliotrope, honesty, honeysuckle, hyssop, lucky hand root, mace, mandrake, maple, marjoram, may apple, moonwort, moss, myrtle, nutmeg, oak, oats, onion, orange, pea, pecan, peppermint, periwinkle, pine, pineapple, pipsissewa, poplar, rattlesnake root, rice, sage, sarsaparilla, sassafras, sesame, snakeroot, snakeroot/black, squill, trillium, vervain, vetivert, wheat □

MOON BLESSINGS: almond, cherry, willow

NATURE SPELLS: magnolia

NEGATIVITY: BANISH: cinquefoil, clove, patchouli, sage

SKILLS: angelica, anise, bay, borage, cinnamon, fennel, mugwort

STRENGTH: ginger, ginseng, lemongrass

RIGHT THINKING: Buddhist temple blend

RITUAL: ADD ENERGY: carnation

TOOLS-CONSECRATE: cypress, rose, sage

RUNE MAGICK: bracken

SAMHAIN: dandelion

SCRYING: fennel, mugwort

SEX: beets patchouli, sandalwood, yohimbe, ylang-ylang

SPIRITS: angelica, nutmeg, wormwood

THIEVES PROTECT FROM: agave prickly pear cactus, thistle

TRIPLE GODDESS: rue, trefoil-clover, wild pansy, wood avens

TRIUMPH: laurel, oak leaves

VAMPIRES-REPEL: garlic

WINTER INCENSE: pine

WOMAN'S LOVE-ATTRACT: henbane, musk, rose

BREWS

For a basic brew, it's pretty easy. You can use fresh or dried. Either way, gather, grind, and mix them. As you mix them, concentrate on your goal, be it of a magickal or non-magickal nature.

Heat a couple cups of water to a boil, and pour over the herbs in the teapot. Cover the tea pot, and let the herbs brew for about 13 minutes. Strain through cheesecloth, metal tea sieve, or a bamboo strainer, and drink, or use as directly.

Solar teas and infusions are made slightly differently: for a solar tea, put the herbs or fruits into a jar filled with water, and let it sit in the sun for as many hours as possible. For certain infusions, you will need to boil the herbs along with the water in the tea kettle, and pour the results into a strainer. Some bark, roots, and dried fruits take longer to infuse than others, hence the need to boil the herbs with the water.

BASICS OF BREWMASTERY

A "brew", as used in this book, indicates an infusion, decoction, potion, or tea. Most of the herbs listed in the previous section can be ingested, but there are a couple exceptions. BEFORE YOU INGEST ANY HERB, MAKE SURE IT IS NOT POISONOUS! You can do this over the web, of course, or with any reputable herbal medicine dictionary or encyclopedia.

That said, brews are a wonderfully inexpensive and natural way to cure ailments of the body, mind, and spirit. Many pharmaceuticals are based on herbs and plants that you could easily grow at home! It seems a shame to give money to Big Pharma when you could just cultivate your own medicinal garden.

WATER

The type of water used when making a brew to be ingested is important. Well, spring, filtered, and distilled waters are preferred, but be wary of bottled waters. Not all bottled waters are created equal.

Tap water, in many areas, far surpasses the quality of 2/3rds of the bottled waters out there. No joke—there are no federal regulations, and few state regulations, on bottled water, and plenty of regulations on tap water. Have you ever heard of any American dying from consuming tap water? Never, right? Despite the bad rap that tap water gets, it's among the safest water in the world.

Also, bottled water creates ridiculous amounts of non-biodegradable waste. Every piece of plastic ever produced still exists in some landfill somewhere. And another important point to remember is that plastic comes from oil. Don't get me started on the dangers of oil dependency, both foreign and domestic. So to make a long story short: getting a Brita filter and filtering your tap water will give you water that is just as good as most bottled waters out there, and will cause less waste and less pollution.

HEATING THE BREW

Putting a kettle on a stove or over a fire is your best bet. I guess you could prepare a brew in a microwave oven, but this isn't the best idea. It could be in my head, but somehow, I feel like foods and liquids heated in a microwave just don't taste as good.

TOOLS AND VESSELS

You don't need much to make a good brew: you'll just want a good quality tea kettle, a tea pot, and a clear jar for solar or lunar teas. Some prefer to dry and prepare the herbs themselves, in which case you may find a mortar and pestle handy. You'll probably want to consecrate and purify each of your tools before you use them.

RECIPES

Aphrodite Lust Drink

2 tsp. Black Tea

1 pinch Coriander

3 fresh Mint leaves (or 1/2 tsp. dried)

5 fresh Rosebud petals (or 1 tsp. dried)

½ tsp dried lemon peel

1 pinch Nutmeg

3 pieces Orange peel

Place all ingredients into teapot. Boil three cups or so of water and add to the pot. Sweeten with honey or maple syrup.

Venus Lust Drink

5 parts Rose petals

1/2 part Clove

1/2 part Nutmeg

1 part ginger

1 tsp honey (to taste)

Make as a normal tea.

Chakra Opening Brew

3 parts Rose petals

1 part Cinnamon

1/2 part Nutmeg

½ part clove

½ part black tea

Place in teapot, fill with boiling water, let steep, covered, for a few minutes. Let it steep and then drink with honey, if desired.

Sweet Dreams Tea

1 part chamomile

1 part lavender

½ part spearmint (not peppermint)

Mix and let steep until cool enough to drink. Then drink before bed.

Headache Brew

1 pinch White Willow bark

1 pinch peppermint

1 lemon wedge

Brew and drink a half a cup as needed. Can be used daily. DO NOT TAKE IF YOU ARE PREGNANT OR LACTATING.

Sleep Brew

1 part chamomile

1 part lavender

1 part valerian

Drink one cup before bed.

ROSEMARY TEA

Useful for: general aches and pains, lack of energy

Directions: boil water, and add one teaspoon of crushed or dried rosemary. Pour through a strainer and serve. Honey may be used as a sweetener

GINGER TEA

Useful for: asthma, respiratory problems

Directions: add ¼ teaspoon of ginger to ½ cup of hot water. Take two tablespoons before bedtime.

HOLY BASIL TEA

Useful for: chronic bronchitis; chronic irritation of the upper respiratory tract

1 tablespoon of basil
2 cups of hot water.

Directions: Take two tablespoons four times per day

CINNAMON TEA

Useful for: congestion; common cold

3 g. bark
1 ½ cups of hot water.

Directions: Steep and drink at bedtime as tea.

CAYENNE PEPPER SHOT

Useful for: extreme congestion, sinus infection

1 c. hot water.
1 tsp lemon juice
1 garlic clove put through a garlic press
1 pinch cayenne pepper.

Directions: Mix well and take as a shot.

FENNEL LINSEED TEA

Useful for: constipation

1/3 tsp Fennel seeds, powdered
1/3 tsp Linseed seeds, powdered
1/3 tsp Liquorice root, powdered
1 3/4 cups Water

Combine equal quantities of the three herbs and add this herb mixture to the water and boil, covered, for 10 minutes. Filter the tea before drinking.

Dosage: 1 cup, 3 times a day.

BLACK PEPPER TEA

Useful for: diarrhea

5 crushed pepper seeds
1 c. water

Directions: Boil the seeds in the water for 15 minutes in a covered container. Remove from the heat and strain. Take 1/2 tea spoon, twice a day.

GINGER MINT TEA

Useful for: fever

2g crushed ginger
2g crushed mint leaves
1 1/2 c. hot water

Directions: Mix the 2 herbs in the water and bring to a boil. Cover and cook for 15 minutes. Strain the decoction and drink.

LEMON TEA

Useful for: cold, fever

1 lemon slice
1 cup hot water

Directions: bring water to a boil. Pour a cup and add the lemon slice. Sip slowly.

YARROW TEA

Useful for: piles

1-2 tea spoon Herb/blossoms, crushed
1 cup Water

Directions: prepare the infusion by combining the herb with the water in a covered container. Let the mixture stand for 5-6 hours. Strain before drinking.

CORIANDER INFUSION

Useful for: impotence

1 tsp of chopped coriander leaves
1 cup of boiling water

To make the infusion, cover the leaves with boiling water,
Close the lid of the teapot and leave for 15 minutes, then
strain.

Dosage: 2-4 table spoon a day.

Remember: coriander leaf extract acts as an aphrodisiac,
while Coriander seed extract suppresses the sex drive.

MINT TEA

Useful for: stomach pain

1 tea spoon spearmint leaves, crushed
2 cups Water

Combine the spearmint leaves and the water and raise the mixture to a boil in a covered container. Remove from the heat and let the tea stand for 15 minutes. Strain before drinking.

Dosage: 1-2 cups a day.

GINGER INFUSION

Useful for: painful menstruation

6 g Embelia, whole plant, powdered
6 g Ginger, dried, powdered
1 3⁄4 cups Water
6 g Sugar

Mix the two herbs and boil. Remove from the heat, strain and sweeten with the sugar.

Dosage: 3⁄4 cup a day.

ONION COLD RELIEF

Useful for: extreme congestion; chest colds

1 onion, sliced

Merely keep the sliced onion by the bed of a person who is suffering from horrific chest congestion. A personal testimonial: I once was so sick that I couldn't sleep unless I was sitting up. Otherwise I would be overcome with wracking coughs. I tried everything: codeine, robitussin, liquor, lemon juice, a cayenne pepper shot, a chest rub...nothing worked. I could not sleep. Finally I received a suggestion to slice an onion and leave it by my bed. My room smelled for three days, but I was finally able to sleep peacefully.

NATURAL FLU RELIEF

Useful for: relief from the flu

2 teaspoons cayenne pepper

1 ½ teaspoons salt

1 cup hot chamomile tea

1 cup apple cider vinegar

Juice from 1 lemon slice

Make chamomile tea. While it is steeping, grind the cayenne pepper and salt together. Add the hot chamomile tea, let it cool, and then add the vinegar. Take a tablespoon or so every half hour.

Potions, Incense, Oils & Ointments

INCENSE

Incense can be extremely useful in magickal workings, and just to have in the home in order to purify or sweeten the energy of a space. Though such purification isn't usually necessary, it can really help the practitioner get in the right state of focus. The herbs and scents used in incense should be chosen carefully. When the incense burns, the energies of the burning or smoldering herbs and various ingredients alter the energy of the room or space. It is important to have it altered in the right manner. If you are burning incense or a scented candle merely to sweeten the smell of a place, choosing a scent that is merely aesthetically pleasing to you is fine.

HOW IS INCENSE MADE?

Incenses are composed of a variety of leaves, flowers, roots, barks, woods, resins, and oils, usually mixed with some form of gunpowder or salt peter to keep the fire smoldering. There are some very common herbs and oils that can be easily kept around the house so that you can make incense whenever you wish. Handy ingredients would include:

Frankincense
Rose petals
Bay
Cloves
Cinnamon
Sandalwood
Basil
Rosemary
Cedar

Remember that a substance may smell very different when it is burning. Think of tobacco—raw tobacco is very sweet, but when burned, quickly takes on an acrid, bitter smell.

There are two main kinds of incense—combustible and not combustible. Combustible incense can be burned in the form cones and sticks, whereas noncombustible incense must be sprinkled onto glowing charcoal to release its fragrance. Both are fairly easy to make at home.

A note about safety: incense can cause a fire if left unattended. If you routinely work with candles and incense, make sure that there is no long fabric or drapes or anything flammable that could possibly fall on or in the flame. It's also a good idea to have a fire extinguisher handy, or, at the very least, a large bowl of water nearby so that you can take action if things go wrong. Never let pets or children wander around near fire or incense unless you are watching closely. Thousands of homes burn down every year because of candles, smoldering cigarettes, and incense. It can happen to you, too, if you're not careful!

That said, responsible use of fire, candles, and incense can be a great addition to any home, magickal or non magickal. Though making your own incense is time consuming, messy, and kind of a pain given that it can be purchased so cheaply, some feel that there is a certain satisfaction in hand-picking the ingredients and making the scents at home. Personally, I would love to make my own incense but since there are so many hours in the day, I just buy mine. Purists, however, may want to make their own.

NONCOMBUSTIBLE INCENSE

This is the easiest to make by far, so you may want to get started with noncombustible before venturing into creating combustible incense. Before you start, make sure that each ingredient has been ground very finely. You can use a mortar and pestle, or a rolling pin, or a special electric grinder reserved for incense making.

When everything has been ground, take a large wooden or ceramic bowl and mix the resins and gums together with your hands.

Next, mix in all the powdered leaves, barks, flowers and roots
 Now add any oils or liquids that are included in the recipe.

Charge and empower the incense and it is done.

Store in a tightly capped jar. Label carefully, including the name of the incense and date of composition.

COMBUSTIBLE INCENSE

Combustible incense requires gum tragacanth glue or mucilage so that the powder will stick enough to be made into a cone, or adhered to a small piece of wood. To make tragacanth glue, place a teaspoon of ground tragacanth in a cup of warm water. Whisk it and take away the foam or froth that results with a spoon.

Let the tragacanth absorb the water until it becomes a thick, bitter-smelling paste. Sticks are hard to make, but if you decide to try, the mucilage should be thin. For blocks and cones a thicker mucilage should be made.

If you can't find tragacanth, try using gum Arabic in its place. After you have mixed whatever adhesive you will be using, set it aside to cool. If it gets too viscous, add more warm water and stir it a little.

To make the base of the cone incense, whatever the fragrance, you'll need:

6 parts ground Charcoal (not self-igniting),
1 part ground Benzoin,
2 parts ground Sandalwood,
1 part ground Orris root
6 drops essential oil
2 to 4 parts mixed, incense from one of the below recipes

Mix the first four ingredients until all are well blended. Add the drops of essential oil and mix again with you hands. You can put it in a grinder if you want, just to make sure the particles are fine enough. Then add the incense.

Then using a small kitchen scale, weigh the completed incense and add ten percent potassium nitrate. Mix this until the white powder is thoroughly blended. Next, add the trag glue, slowly, and mix with your hands. For cone incense you'll need a very stiff, dough-like texture.

On a piece of waxed paper, shape the mixture into basic cone shapes,. When you've made up your cone incense, let it dry for two to seven days in a warm place. Your incense is finished.

INCENSE RECIPES

Aloe and Clove Incense

2 parts Myrrh
1 part Wood Aloe
a few drops clove oil

Burn to contact spirits during rituals or as a simple consecration incense.

Winter Incense

4 parts Benzoin

2 parts Gum Mastic

1 part Violet

1 pinch Wormwood

1 pinch Mistletoe

Burn to invoke the powers of the element of Air

Altar Incense

3 parts Frankincense

2 parts Myrrh

1 part Sage

Burn as a general incense on the altar to purify the area.

Venus Incense

1 part Cinnamon or Clove

1 part Sandalwood

Few drops Cypress or Pine oil

Burn during rituals designed to attract love.

Apollo Incense

4 parts Frankincense

2 parts Myrrh

2 parts Cinnamon

1 part Rosemary

Burn during divination rituals.

AROMATHERAPY MAGICK

"Aromatherapy" is the practice of using the scent of an herb to manipulate the energy in a room or space. While the burning of incense, and the use of ointments and tinctures certainly are a form of aromatherapy, it is also possible to heat essential oils so that their fragrance can be diffused. This way, the scent is pure—unlike incense, perfumes, tinctures, and potions wherein the herb has been blended with other ingredients. Aromatherapy can indicate the practice of inhaling or being exposed to the scent of an oil merely by breathing through the nose, or it can be the practice of using the oils in massage or bathing.

Ideally, the oils should be carefully selected. They are the essence of a plant or herb, and are highly concentrated. They contain hormones, vitamins, and antiseptics that work on both the spiritual and mental bodies. Not

Essential oils are very potent, and it is important to make sure that you are not allergic to any oils that you may be putting on your skin. When using essential oils, use the smallest amount of essential oils that will get the job done. If one drop will get the job done, for example, don't use two drops. For therapeutic results, purchase only high quality oils, and remember not to take them internally, even if they are from a food (such as mango or strawberry oil).

Aromatherapy has many benefits. Merely the scent of certain herbs can aid in relaxation, pain, aid memory, relieve cold symptoms, and contribute to the well-being of a space or a person.

The oils are taken from the herb or plant in a variety of ways. Citrus essential oils, such as bergamot, clementine, tangerine, sweet orange, lemon, grapefruit, lime, and mandarin, are usually cold-pressed from the peels. Most other essential oils are steam distilled, a process which not only separates the essential oil from the plant. In some cases, solvent extraction, is used. In this process, the plant is treated with a solvent that attracts the essential oil molecules. The solvent is then disposed of.

THE OLFACTORY SYSTEM

Our sense of smell is one of our most primitive. It is linked with emotions, and in fact, our memory of scent is longer lasting and more accurate than our memory of sight. Scent can cause our stress level and heart rate to rise or fall, and can influence our digestive systems. Essential oils' fragrance molecules travel to the brain through the breathing process, and effect us immediately.

Essential Oils absorbed topically (through the skins pores) reach the bloodstream through connective and lymphatic tissues. This is effective, however, it takes longer than through the process of smell.

THE GUIDE TO PROPER SELECTION OF ESSENTIAL OILS

Though certain spells call for particular oils, you can use oils at your discretion to promote or capture a certain mood. Here is a list of oils and their corresponding properties.

To Aid Memory Recall, Sharpen the Mental State

Cedar wood, Marjoram, Peppermint, Rosemary

To Provide a Relaxing Atmosphere, Assist in Sleep

Chamomile, Clary Sage, Eucalyptus, Juniper Berry, Lavender, Mandarin, Marjoram, Neroli, Rose, Rose Geranium.

To Aid in Achieving Mental Alertness

Black Pepper, Cayenne Pepper, Grapefruit, Juniper Berry, Lemon, Peppermint, Pine, Rosemary, Ylang Ylang.

To Soothe Anxiety

Chamomile, Clary Sage, Eucalyptus, Juniper Berry, Lavender, Petitgrain, Rosemary, Sandalwood.

To Ease Congestion

Eucalyptus, Ginger, Lavender, Lemon, Patchouli, Peppermint, Pepper, Pine, Rosemary.

To Relieve Physical Pain:

Chamomile, Ginger, Helichrysum, Lavender, Marjoram, Rosemary, Rose.

USEFUL OILS

Oils, in my opinion, are an indispensable part of practicing Magick, much less necessary for a well-kept and pleasant home environment. They are, however, admittedly rather expensive. So here is a list of the oils that are the most useful, the least expensive, and the best to have on hand.

Lavender:

Known to be calming, this oil is often used for insomnia. It makes an excellent addition to pillows, sachets, and baths. It's also good for general first aid, burns, bites.

Tea Tree:

This is an almost essential part of any first aid cabinet. The uses of Tea Tree oil are almost limitless. It is antibacterial, antiviral and antifungal, and be used to treat cuts, bites, dandruff, and athletes foot. It is extremely potent, but can be used without distillation or dilution. Care should be taken to keep it from children, and to be careful when using it on sensitive skin.

Eucalyptus:

This is an excellent oil to have around for people who suffer from frequent colds, sinus problems, or congestion. Diffusing the scent can help break up congestion, and it is particularly effective when mixed with peppermint.

Peppermint

Peppermint can soothe headaches, act as a digestive aid, and ease travel sickness. Use in massage, a cold compress, in a diffuser, or as an inhalant. It also energizes, and reduces nausea.

Orange

Orange, or its more expensive counterparts of Bergamot and Mandarin, is uplifting.

Lemon

Lemon is great for cleaning, and studies have shown that a lemon-scented environment encourages others to be more diligent about cleaning up after themselves!

RECIPES

Here are some simple recipes using essential oils:

Invigorating Oil Mix

Energizing Oil

4 oz. Sweet Almond Oil

30 drops Sweet Orange essential oil

15 drops Lemon essential oil

10 drops Lime essential oil

10 drops Grapefruit essential oil

10 drops Bergamot essential oil

This recipe makes a wonderfully refreshing and lightly energizing Oil. Be careful if you have sensitive skin!

OINTMENT MAGICK

Ointments are not made to be ingested, but to be used on your body, or on candles or other magickal objects for the purposes of anointment. If you want the ointment to be waxy, you can mix the oils with beeswax. If you merely wish to add volume, use a carrier oil like grapeseed or apricot kernel oil.

Exorcism Ointment

3 drops Frankincense
2 drops Peppermint
1 drop Clove
1 drop Sage

Add the oils to the beeswax/oil base.

Flying Ointment, Nontoxic #2

2 drops Sandalwood Oil

1 drop Jasmine Oil

1 drop Benzoin Oil

1 drop Mace Oil

Add the oils to the beeswax/oil base. Use as the above formula.

Back to the top

Chest Cold Ointment

4 drops Cedar wood

1 drop Eucalyptus

1 drop Cinnamon

1 drop Pepper oil or pinch of cayenne pepper

Add to the melted beeswax/oil base, cool, and anoint the body to speed healing as needed. Do not apply to wounds, burns or broken skin!

Love Ointment

4 drops Bergamot

2 drops Rose

2 drop Vanilla extract

1 drop Cardamom

Make in the usual way and anoint the body when looking for love.

Moon Goddess Ointment

2 drops patchouli

2 drops Lemon

1 drop Rose

1 drop Amber

Prepare with the beeswax/oil base. Anoint yourself to attune with the Goddess of the Moon.

Sun God Ointment

4 drops Frankincense

3 drops Orange

1 drop Cinnamon

1 drop Ginger

Make and mix with carrier oil or beeswax.

Youth Ointment

2 parts Rose

1 part Grapefruit

Add to beeswax or carrier oil .

HONEY ELIXER

1 tsp sage

1 tsp thyme

1 tsp spearmint

Boil in two cups of spring water and once it reaches a rolling boil add:

1 tsp cider vinegar

3 ounces of honey

mix well, and cool.

Store in an amber bottle if you wish to drink the rest later.

TINCTURE MAGICK

Tinctures are used for anointment and aromatherapy, and should not be ingested! Furthermore, use with caution until you make sure that you aren't allergic to any of the ingredients in a tincture. People with sensitive skill should be particularly cautious.

Oils are widely used in magic to stimulate consciousness through the olfactories, and tinctures are just as effective. In magickal perfumery, a tincture is created by soaking dried plant materials in alcohol. It is very easy to do, and much cheaper than purchasing tinctures on line or at herbal medicine type stores. Plus, you can make your own tinctures and refine your own recipes.

MAKING TINCTURES

For tincturing you need an alcohol of at least 70 percent strength, or 140 proof. Vodka, unfortunately, isn't strong enough.

You will also need dried herbs, fruits, or plants. The not-dried ones won't work! To dry a plant hang it upside down in the sun, or just lay it in the windowsill where it can get the sun's rays. If the climate is too humid or the sun too weak, the herbs may just rot. So experiment with where you place the herbs and at what time of day.

Next, empower and consecrate the herb, and then pour into a small, amber or dark bottle with a tight-fitting lid. Using a small funnel, pour just enough ethyl alcohol into the bottle to wet and cover the herb. Cap tightly. Shake the bottle vigorously every day for a week or two.

Then, using a coffee filter, strain the alcohol. If it's not strong enough, add more herbs and enough alcohol to cover them.

To correctly determine whether the tincture is properly scented, apply a drop or two to your wrist. Wait until the alcohol has evaporated and then smell your wrist. Remember, each scent smells differently on people because it combines with their pheromones in different ways. That's why it's important to try perfumes before you buy them, and let them sit on your skin for at least an hour to see how they mix with your natural scent. Even if one doesn't mix well with your scent, however, you can use it on sachets, pillows, or other household objects, or for anointing magickal objects.

After you have tested the smell of your tincture and you are satisfied, filter it one last time through the coffee filter, and add a few drops of castor oil or glycerin. Store in an amber bottle in a cool place for future use.

POPULAR TINCTURES

Guardian Tincture

Cinnamon
Cedar
Clove

Anoint yourself or objects for protection.

Mind Clearing Tincture

Sage
Thyme
Rosemary

Anoint your body and healing amulets with this tincture.

Love Tincture

Orange peel
Rose Petals
Vanilla bean

Sacred Tincture

Frankincense
Myrrh

Cinnamon Tincture

Cinnamon

Cinnamon has such a distinctive, strong, sweet smell that it makes an excellent tincture on its own, and can be combined with other ointments for different smells.

Clove Tincture

Clove

Cloves too are strong enough and rich enough to be used alone.

Sage Tincture

Sage

This earthy, musky smell is just fine on its own.

Sleep Well Tincture

Lavender
Chamomile

This can be used in a sachet or a pillow to promote restful sleep and good dreams.

Nutmeg Tincture

Nutmeg

This tincture can be used alone, and can be smelled to wake up the senses, or can be used in money spells.

Peppermint Tincture

Peppermint

This mint-green tincture is used in money, purification and love rituals. Anoint sleep pillows. Try spearmint, too.

Wake Up Tincture

Cinnamon
Clove
Nutmeg
Pepper

This heady scent is perfect to wake up to.

Oily Skin Application

½ aloe gel

1 tbsp witch hazel

1 1/2 tsp cornstarch

3-4 drop peppermint essential oil

Mix the aloe, witch hazel, and cornstarch. Heat over a flame or even in the microwave, if you must, stirring every 20 seconds. When it turns into a clear gel-like substance, it is ready. Remove from heat. Keep stirring as it cools. The cornstarch will turn a clear aloe gel to an almost white cream color. Then add the peppermint. Store in an amber bottle. This can be applied to oily skin daily,.

BATH MAGICK WITH OILS AND HERBS

The bath can be an excellent place to put together your knowledge of herbs and oils. Ritual baths are, of course, necessary to prepare for many spells and Magickal workings. They can also be a great way to relax, or Magickal workings in and of themselves. Before using any herbs or oils in the bath, however, make sure that you're not allergic to them! Bathwater can creep into some pretty sensitive areas, and the last thing you want is to irritate sensitive parts of the skin!

Protection Bath

You will need:

1 tsp basil
1 cup boiling spring water

Steep a teaspoon of basil in a cup of boiling water, and strain out the herb. Add it to the bathwater, and enjoy!

Lavender Bath

You will need:

Lavender colored candle
1 tsp lavender flowers
1 tsp chamomile flowers
1 tsp rosemary
1 tbsp lemon juice
1 square foot of muslin or cheesecloth
lavender ribbon

To begin, cast a circle in your bathroom. Call the elements, and light the candle. Then blend the herbs, and put them in the fabric. Tie the fabric using a ribbon so that you have made a little sachet. Put it in the bathwater, and then add the lemon juice.

When you settle into the tub, lean back, relax, and take three deep breaths. Meditate and relax.

Lavender Bath Salts

1⁄2 cup sea salt

1⁄4 cup Epsom salts

1⁄4 cup dead sea mineral salts

40 drops lavender essential oil

Mix all ingredients well, then add the essential oil. Use one half cup for your bath. To begin, cast a circle. Then add the bath salt as the water fills the tub.

When you enter the tub, center yourself, and meditate.

Healing Bath

You will need:

¼ cup dead sea salts
1 tsp dried lavender
5 drops lavender oil.
Muslin sachet

Fill your muslin bag half way with the dead sea salts, add two teaspoons of lavender herb
and one drop of lavender oil. Tie up the bag and include in your bath. As you slide in to the tub, relax and visualize any aches, pains, or negative energy being lifted from you, and away.

Bath Bomb

You will need:

4 cups Epsom salts
2 cups Sea salt
1 cup non fat powdered milk
2 cups oatmeal ground to a very fine powder in blender or
food processor.
40 drops of essential oil

Bath bombs are delightfully fizzy, and make any bath a
pleasure. If you wish to relax in the bath, I'd advocate
choosing lavender, violet, or chamomile essential oil. Mix
everything together, put it through a sieve, and then add
the oil. Add it slowly--10 drops at a time, and mix it. Add it
to your bath and enjoy!

Sinus Relief Bath

You will need

1/2 cup each of dried yarrow flowers

½ dried mint leaves

½ cup dried rose petals.

½ cup comfrey leaves

1 tbsp lemon juice

Place the herbs in muslin, cheesecloth or nylon. Tie it off and let it steep in the bath for a few minutes, like a giant tea bag. You can use the bundle to exfoliate as well.

Cleansing and Purifying Bath

You will need

½ cup dried rose petals.

1 T bicarbonate soda

5 drops essential oil

1 tsp. almond or apricot kernel oil

 ½ cup sea salt

Stir the soda, essential oil, lemon juice and oil together and then blend in the salt.

Dissolve in the bath water. Call the elements, cast a circle, and place candles at the 4 corners of the tub.

Step slowly into the bath water, feeling it envelope around you. Close your eyes. Say, aloud or to yourself:

All is well, all is blessed

Time in here is time for rest

Fly away on swift wings

Aches, pains, evil things.

Mental Rejuvenation Bath

You will need

10 drops almond oil

10 drops cypress oil,

10 drops lavender oil.

4 blue candles

Anoint your hand with sandalwood oil and skim your hand over the surface of the water four times.

Then enter the bath and meditate away any sources of mental or physical stress.

Bath For Muscle Aches

You will need:

2 tsp dried thyme (This herb is a great muscle relaxant.)

2 tsp dried rosemary

2 tsp lavender

2 tsp Epsom salt

bath sachet or muslin, cheesecloth, or nylon bag.

Mix the herbs and place in the cloth or bath sachet. Soak as long as you need so as to do away with muscle aches and pains.

CANDLE MAGICK

Candle magick is a very powerful form of magick. Candles are a part of most spells and incantations, and understanding how to properly use candles is an important part of Wicca.

Flame is, obviously, fire energy. When you use a candle, your work will be infused with fire energy. Selecting the appropriate color candle will help you focus the nature of the energy.

White

* The Goddess
* Higher Self
* Purity
* Peace
* Cleanliness

Black

* Binding
* Shape shifting
* Protection

* Shields from negative spirits

Brown

* friendship

Silver

* goddess energy
* Astral energy
* Female energy
* Night energy
* Intuition
* Dreams

Purple

* Third Eye
* Psychic Ability
* Hidden Knowledge
* Spiritual Power

Blue

* Water energy
* Protection

* Calm
* Good Fortune
* Communication
* Spiritual Inspiration

Green

* Earth energy
* Physical Healing
* Prosperity
* Tree and Plant Magic
* Growth

Pink

* Romantic love
* Romance
* Affection
* Nurturing

Red

* magnifies fire energy
* Passion
* Strength
* decisiveness

* Lust
* Aggression
* Survival
* Sexual energy
* Masculine energy

Orange

* Spiritual Success
* Property Deals
* Friendship
* Justice

Gold

* God energy
* Promote Winning
* Male energy
* Happiness
* Exuberance
* Sun energy

Yellow

* The Element of Air
* Intelligence

* Logic

It is also possible to manipulate the color of the flame using the following chemicals:

Green flame: Borax or Boric acid, copper nitrates or barium nitrates
Orange flame: calcium chloride
Red flame: strontium nitrate
Yellow flame: Sodium Chlorate or Potassium Nitrate
Purple flame: Lithium Chlorate

To change the flame of a Fire: Put three level spoons of the chemical into a paper cup; fill 1/2 full with water and stir. Soak several small chips of wood in this solution overnight. The next day, remove the chips with tweezers and lay on newspaper to dry. They can now be added to your fireplace to produce bright colors.

To change the flame of the candle: when you make the candle, the wicks will have to be soaked in the chemical. Three level spoons of the chemical should be mixed in ½ water, and the wicks should soak in it and then dry. Be careful if you have sensitive skin!

www.ingramcontent.com/pod-product-compliance
Lightning Source LLC
LaVergne TN
LVHW091154080426
835509LV00006B/676